SHARK FRENZY

Angel Sharks

by Rebecca Pettiford

BLASTOFF! READERS 3

BELLWETHER MEDIA • MINNEAPOLIS, MN

Blastoff! Readers are carefully developed by literacy experts to build reading stamina and move students toward fluency by combining standards-based content with developmentally appropriate text.

Level 1 provides the most support through repetition of high-frequency words, light text, predictable sentence patterns, and strong visual support.

Level 2 offers early readers a bit more challenge through varied sentences, increased text load, and text-supportive special features.

Level 3 advances early-fluent readers toward fluency through increased text load, less reliance on photos, advancing concepts, longer sentences, and more complex special features.

★ **Blastoff! Universe**

Reading Level

Grade **K**

Grades **1–3**

Grade **4**

This edition first published in 2021 by Bellwether Media, Inc.

No part of this publication may be reproduced in whole or in part without written permission of the publisher. For information regarding permission, write to Bellwether Media, Inc., Attention: Permissions Department, 6012 Blue Circle Drive, Minnetonka, MN 55343.

Library of Congress Cataloging-in-Publication Data

Names: Pettiford, Rebecca, author.
Title: Angel sharks / by Rebecca Pettiford.
Description: Minneapolis, MN : Bellwether Media, [2021] | Series: Blastoff! Readers: Shark frenzy | Includes bibliographical references and index. | Audience: Ages 5-8 | Audience: Grades 2-3 | Summary: "Simple text and full-color photography introduce beginning readers to angel sharks. Developed by literacy experts for students in kindergarten through third grade"-Provided by publisher.
Identifiers: LCCN 2020001599 (print) | LCCN 2020001600 (ebook) | ISBN 9781644872437 (library binding) | ISBN 9781681037066 (ebook)
Subjects: LCSH: Squatinidae–Juvenile literature.
Classification: LCC QL638.95.S88 P48 2021 (print) | LCC QL638.95.S88 (ebook) | DDC 597.3–dc23
LC record available at https://lccn.loc.gov/2020001599
LC ebook record available at https://lccn.loc.gov/2020001600

Editor: Rebecca Sabelko   Designer: Andrea Schneider

Printed in the United States of America, North Mankato, MN.

Table of Contents

What Are Angel Sharks?

Pacific angel shark

Angel sharks are flat-bodied sharks. They look like they have wings!

Angel sharks are found all over the world. They live in warm coastal waters. These **carnivores** hunt along the sandy ocean floor.

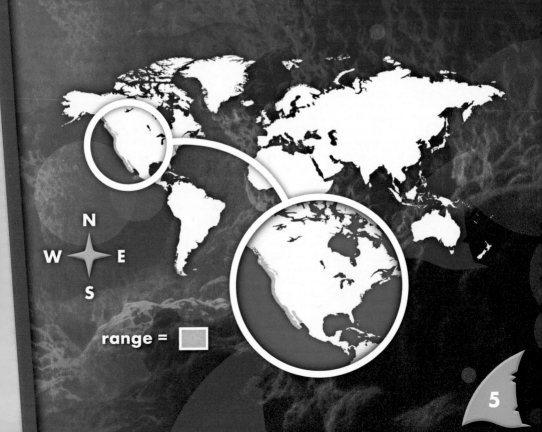

Pacific Angel Shark Range

N
W · E
S

range = ▢

There are many **species** of angel sharks. Most are about 5 feet (1.5 meters) long. Some reach 8 feet (2.4 meters) long!

Shark Sizes

average human

common angel shark

6 feet (2 meters) long •‒

up to 8 feet (2.4 meters) long

Angel sharks favor **shallow** waters.
But some species dive deeper.

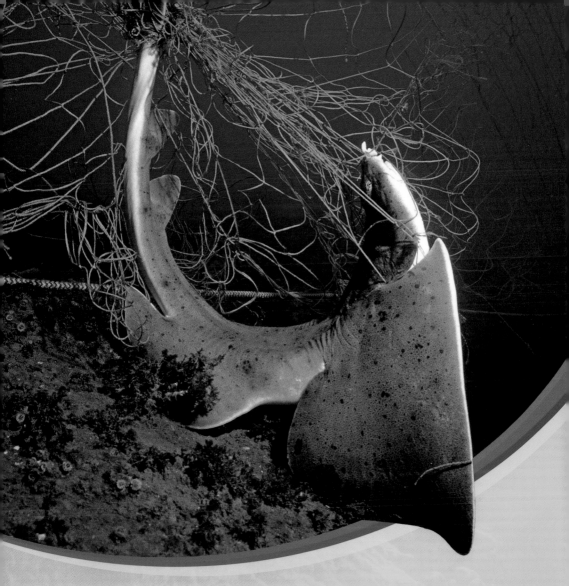

Many species of angel shark are **endangered**. Their **habitats** have been ruined. Overfishing has also killed many angel sharks.

People are working to save them! They report angel shark sightings. They also set limits on fishing.

common angel shark

Angel sharks have gray, brown, or white backs. They are dotted with dark or white spots.

This **camouflage** helps these **bottom-dwellers** hide in the sand and mud.

10

Japanese angel shark

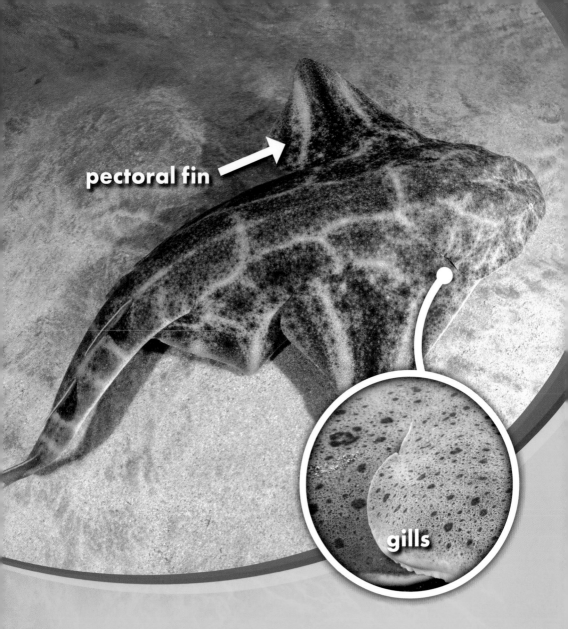

pectoral fin

gills

Wide, flat **pectoral fins** help angel sharks swim. Swimming pushes water through their **gills**. This lets the sharks breathe.

Angel sharks have **spiracles** behind their eyes. These openings help angel sharks breathe when they are under the sand.

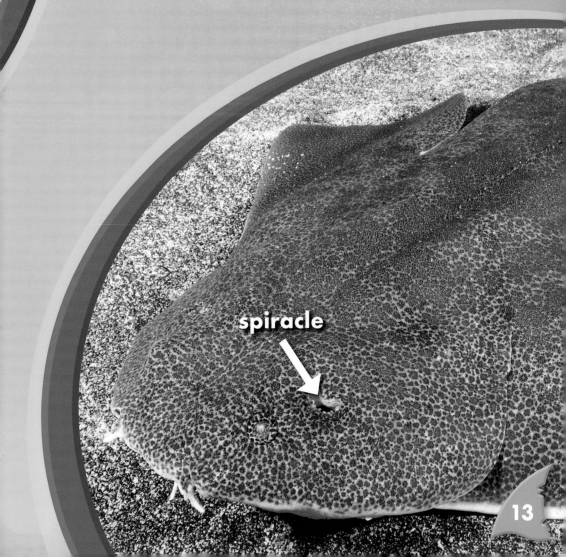

spiracle

Angel sharks have **barbels** on both sides of their mouths. Barbels help the sharks find **prey** on the ocean floor.

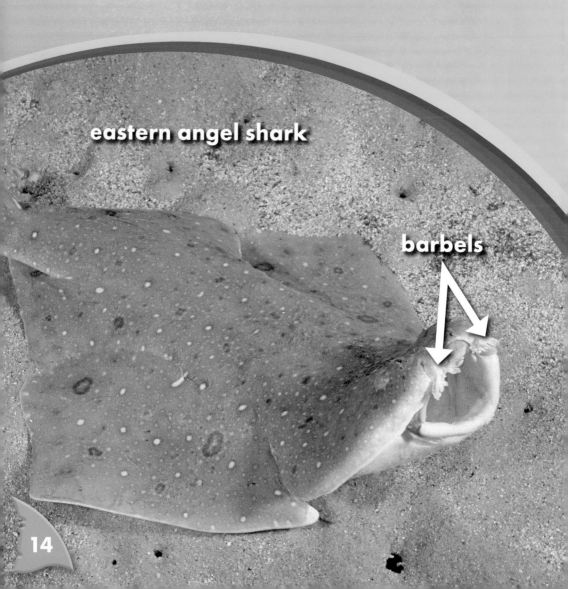

eastern angel shark

barbels

Identify an Angel Shark

barbels

pectoral fins

gills

Their wide jaws have several rows of teeth. These needle-like teeth hold and cut prey.

Angel sharks hide in the sand. These **ambush predators** wait for fish, crabs, and squids to come close.

When prey is near, angel sharks attack! Their powerful jaws suck food into their mouths.

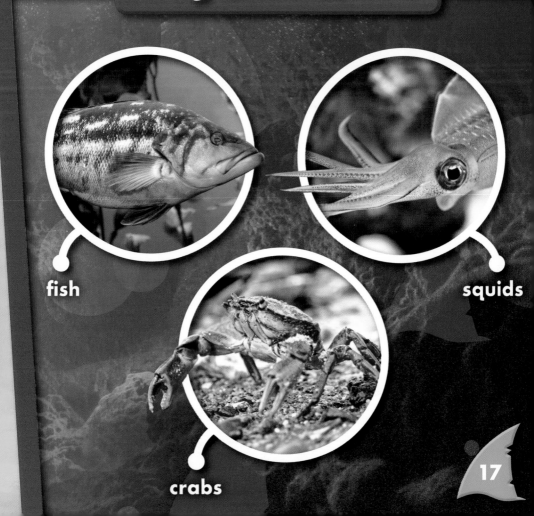

Angel Shark Diet

fish

squids

crabs

Angel sharks face many dangers. Great white sharks and whale sharks hunt them down. People eat them, too.

Angel sharks hide from
danger under the sand!

Deep Dive on the Pacific Angel Shark

LIFE SPAN:
up to 35 years

LENGTH:
up to 5 feet (1.5 meters) long

WEIGHT:
up to 60 pounds (27 kilograms)

DEPTH RANGE:
around 3 to 656 feet (1 to 200 meters)

gills

barbels

pectoral fins

Least Concern	Near Threatened	Vulnerable	Endangered	Critically Endangered	Extinct in the Wild	Extinct

conservation status: near threatened

Glossary

ambush predators—animals that sit and wait to catch their prey; predators are animals that hunt other animals for food.

barbels—whisker-like body parts around the mouths of angel sharks that are used to find food

bottom-dwellers—animals that spend a lot of time on or near the bottom of the ocean

camouflage—a way of using color to blend in with surroundings

carnivores—animals that only eat meat

endangered—animals or plants that are in danger of dying out

gills—parts that help sharks breathe underwater

habitats—lands with certain types of plants, animals, and weather

pectoral fins—a pair of fins on the side of a shark that control a shark's movement

prey—animals that are hunted by other animals for food

shallow—not deep

species—groups of animals or plants that are similar and can reproduce

spiracles—openings behind an angel shark's eyes that are used for breathing

To Learn More

AT THE LIBRARY

Davies, Nicola. *Ocean Monsters: Interact with Lifesize Sea Predators!* London, U.K.: Carlton Books, 2017.

Silverman, Buffy. *Angel Sharks in Action*. Minneapolis, Minn.: Lerner Publications, 2017.

Skerry, Brian. *The Ultimate Book of Sharks: Your Guide to these Fierce and Fantastic Fish*. Washington, D.C.: National Geographic, 2018.

ON THE WEB

FACTSURFER

Factsurfer.com gives you a safe, fun way to find more information.

1. Go to www.factsurfer.com.

2. Enter "angel sharks" into the search box and click 🔍.

3. Select your book cover to see a list of content.

Index

The images in this book are reproduced through the courtesy of: Photoshot/ Superstock, front cover; lophius_sub/ Alamy, p. 3; David Fleetham/ Alamy, pp. 4-5, 12 (gills), 18, 20-21; Carlos Villoch/ Alamy, pp. 6-7; Helmut Corneli/ Alamy, pp. 8-9; Frank Schneider/ Alamy, p. 9; Luis Miguel Estévez/ Dreamstime, p. 10 (inset); Martin Voeller, pp. 10-11; Biosphoto/ Alamy, pp. 12-13; Kelvin Aitken/VWPics/ Alamy, pp. 13, 14-15, 15 (angel shark) (barbels); Nature Picture Library/ Alamy, pp. 16-17; imageBROKER/ Alamy, pp. 17 (fish), 18-19; agefotostock/ Alamy, p. 17 (squids); Harald Schmidt, p. 17 (crabs); Paulo Oliveira/ Alamy, p. 21 (barbels).